World Book, Inc.
180 North LaSalle Street
Suite 900
Chicago, Illinois 60601
USA

For information about other "True or False?" titles, as
well as other World Book print and digital publications,
please go to www.worldbook.com.

For information about other World Book publications,
call 1-800-WORLDBK (967-5325).

For information about sales to schools and libraries,
call 1-800-975-3250 (United States) or 1-800-837-5365
(Canada).

Library of Congress Cataloging-in-Publication Data for
this volume has been applied for.

True or False?
ISBN: 978-0-7166-4069-1 (set, hc.)

Pop Music
ISBN: 978-0-7166-4077-6 (hc.)

Also available as:
ISBN: 978-0-7166 4087-5 (e-book)

Printed in the United States of America by CG Book
Printers, North Mankato, Minnesota

1st printing March 2020

Staff

Executive Committee

President
Geoff Broderick

Vice President, Finance
Donald D. Keller

Vice President, Marketing
Jean Lin

Vice President, International
Maksim Rutenberg

Vice President, Technology
Jason Dole

Director, Content and Product
Development
Tom Evans

Director, Human Resources
Bev Ecker

Editorial

Writers
Shawn Brennan
Jeff De La Rosa

Editor
Mellonee Carrigan

Librarian
S. Thomas Richardson

Manager, Indexing Services
David Pofelski

Digital

Director, Digital Product
Development
Erika Meller

Digital Product Manager
Jonathan Wills

Graphics and Design

Senior Designers
Don Di Sante
Isaiah Sheppard

Senior Visual
Communications Designer
Melanie Bender

Media Editor
Rosalia Bledsoe

Manufacturing/Production

Manufacturing Manager
Anne Fritzinger

Production Specialist
Curley Hunter

Proofreader
Nathalie Strassheim

POP MUSIC

WORLD BOOK

www.worldbook.com

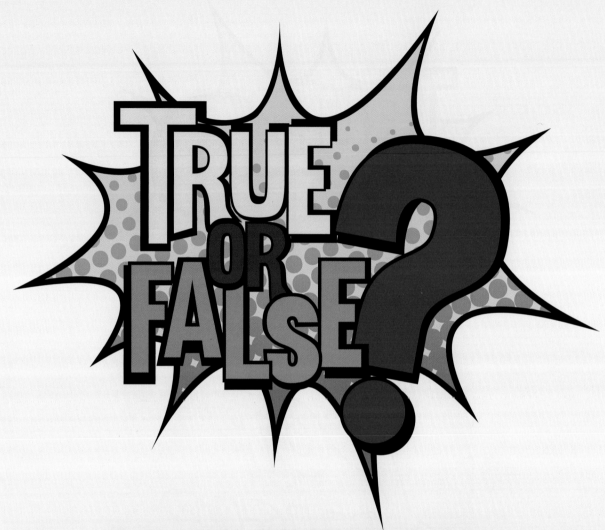

Pop music got its name from advertisers. They noticed that teenagers drank a lot of soda pop while listening to the latest hits on jukeboxes in diners.

Pop music is short for *popular music.*
There are many different styles of
popular music, including blues, country,
gospel, jazz, rap, reggae, rhythm and
blues (R & B), and rock.

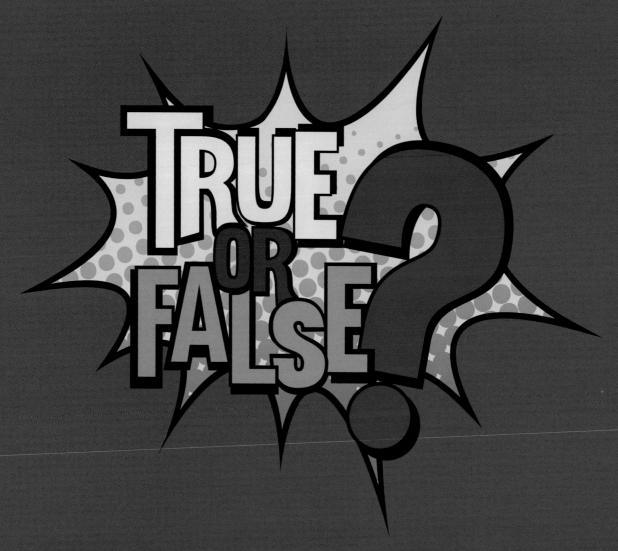

The letters in the name of the *K-pop* (Korean pop) group BTS stand for *Boys to Students.*

BTS originally stood for *Bangtan Sonyeondan*, Korean for *Bulletproof Boy Scouts*. BTS later was said to stand for *Beyond the Scene*.

If you could have streamed music in the mid-1800's, the hottest singles on your playlist would have been written by the American songwriter Stephen Foster.

13

TRUE!

Foster was the most important American songwriter of the mid-1800's. He was the first American to make his living from songwriting. Many of his compositions, such as "Oh! Susanna" (1848) and "Camptown Races" (1850), are still popular today.

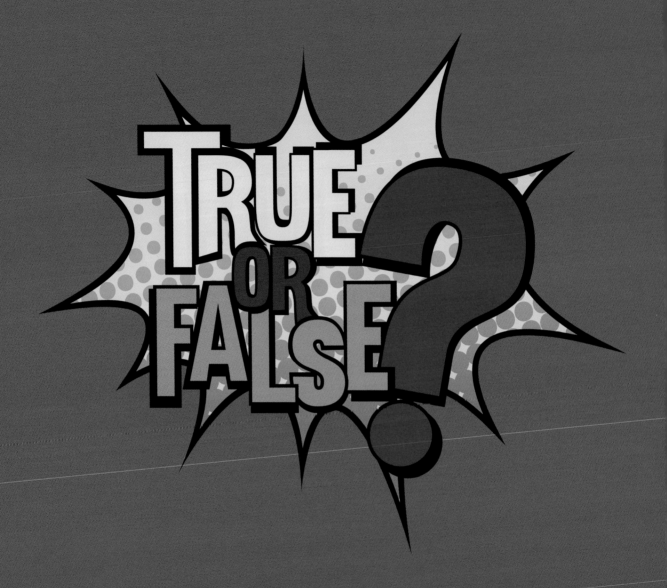

The Beatles were the most popular
group in rock history.

The Beatles, from Liverpool, England, gained nationwide fame in 1962 and worldwide fame in 1964. By the time the Beatles broke up in 1970, their records had outsold those of any other popular music performers in history.

Chance the Rapper became the first musician born in the 2000's to have a number-one album in the United States.

FALSE!

Billie Eilish (born in 2001) became the first musician born in the 2000's to have a number-one album in the United States, with *When We Fall Asleep, Where Do We Go?* (2019). (Chance was born in 1993!)

True or False?

Paul McCartney, formerly of the Beatles, was the first musician to be inducted into the Rock and Roll Hall of Fame three times.

The British musician Eric Clapton was the first musician to be inducted into the Rock and Roll Hall of Fame three times. He was inducted in 1992 as a member of the band the Yardbirds; in 1993 as a member of the band Cream; and in 2000 as a solo artist.

TRUE OR FALSE?

The American pop singer Bruno Mars began his career impersonating the singer Elvis Presley.

29

Mars's real name is Peter Gene Hernandez. He began performing in a local variety show with his family at the age of 4, impersonating the "King of Rock and Roll."

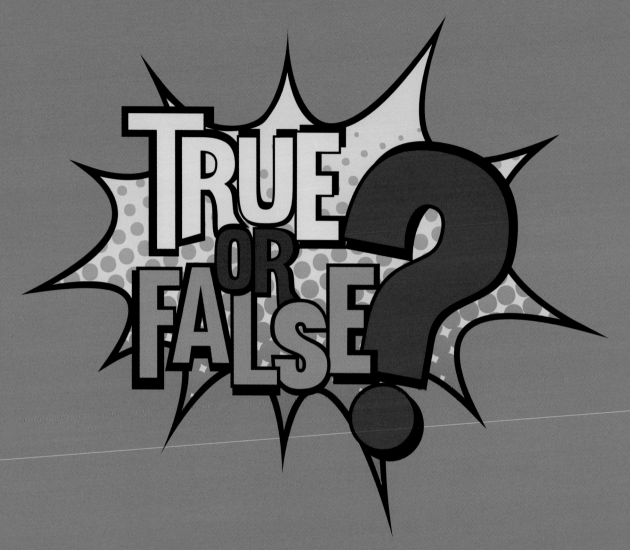

TRUE OR FALSE?

The American singer and actress Jennifer Hudson became famous after appearing on the television show "The Voice."

Hudson gained fame in 2004 as a finalist on the singing competition television show "American Idol."

25

BIGGEST
BUM
ME

Michael Jackson

TRUE OR FALSE?

Michael Jackson's *Thriller* (1982) is the best-selling album in history.

FALSE!

Their Greatest Hits 1971-1975 (1976) by the American rock band the Eagles surpassed *Thriller* in 2018.

ANDERSON EAST

EARTH GIRL HELEN BROWN

EARTH

EAGLES

EAGLES OF DEATH METAL

EAGLES

THEIR GREATEST HITS

39

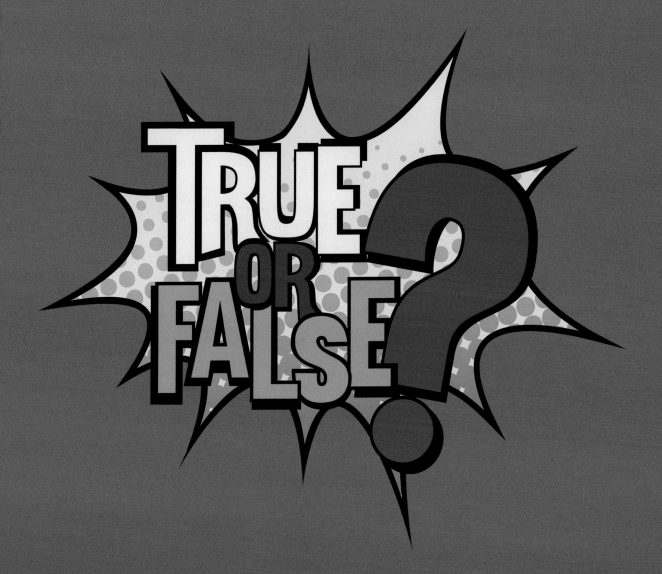

TRUE OR FALSE?

Before the 1920's, new music was "dropped" (released to the public) on paper.

Until the 1920's, popular music was sold mainly through *sheet music*, music printed on loose sheets of paper. The public did the playing (and singing) on their own!

TRUE
OR
FALSE?

The members of the Rolling Stones named their band after their bowling team.

The British rock group, which formed in 1962, took their name from the song "Rollin' Stone" (1950) by the American blues singer Muddy Waters.

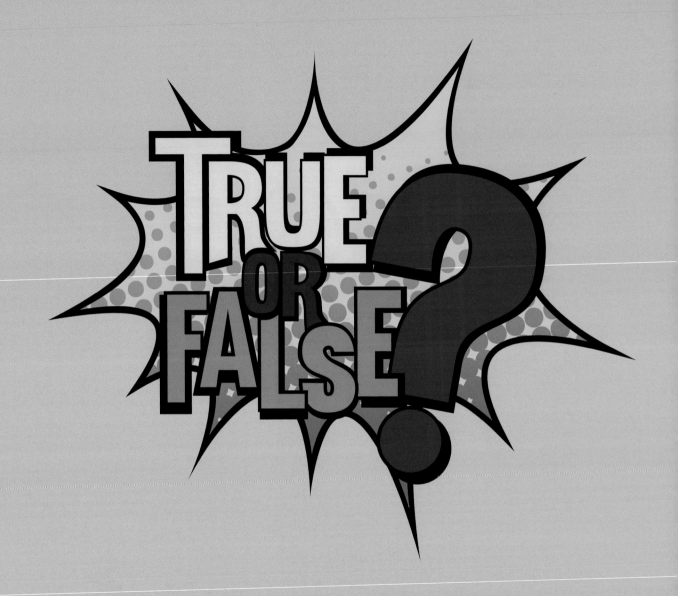

Lady Gaga's stage name was inspired by the British rock group the Babys.

Lady Gaga's real name is Stefani Joanne Angelina Germanotta. Her stage name was inspired by the song "Radio Ga Ga" (1984), by the British rock band Queen.

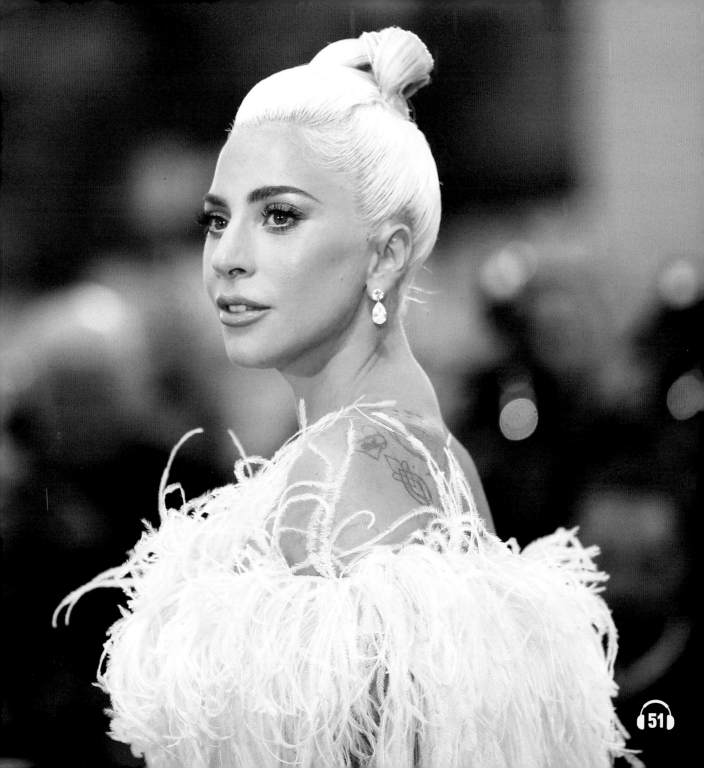

TRUE OR FALSE?

The Mexican American singer Selena became famous for singing the theme song "My Heart Will Go On" from the movie *Titanic* (1997).

53

The French-Canadian singer Céline Dion *(SAY leen dee OHN)* had a hit with "My Heart Will Go On." Selena became a star singing the Tejano style of Hispanic popular music.

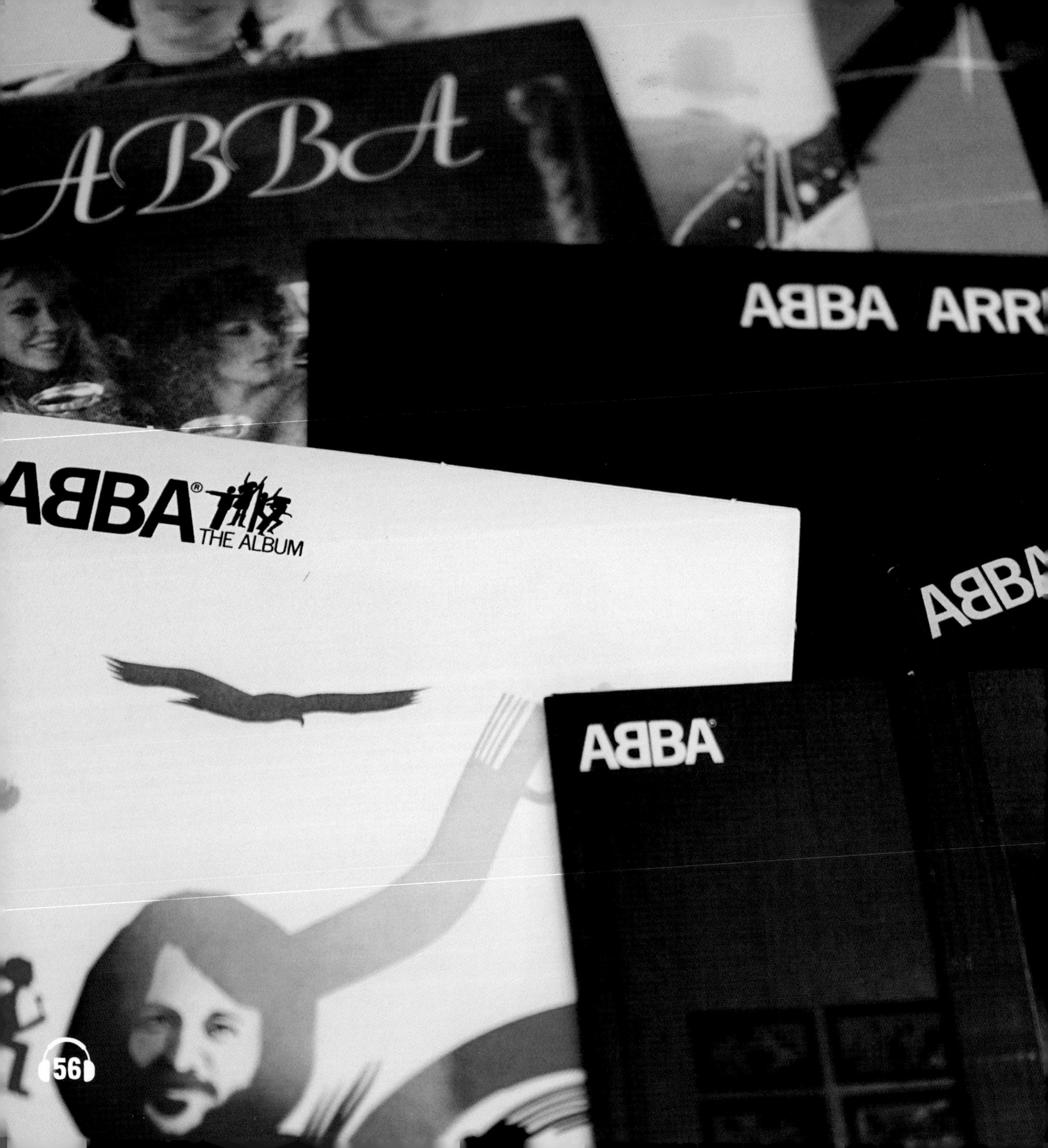
ABBA
ABBA
ABBA®
THE ALBUM
ABBA
ABBA®

The name of the Swedish group
ABBA was taken from the first letter
of each member's first name.

The members of the group were Agnetha Faltskog, Benny Andersson, Bjorn Ulvaeus, and Anni-Frid "Frida" Lyngstad.

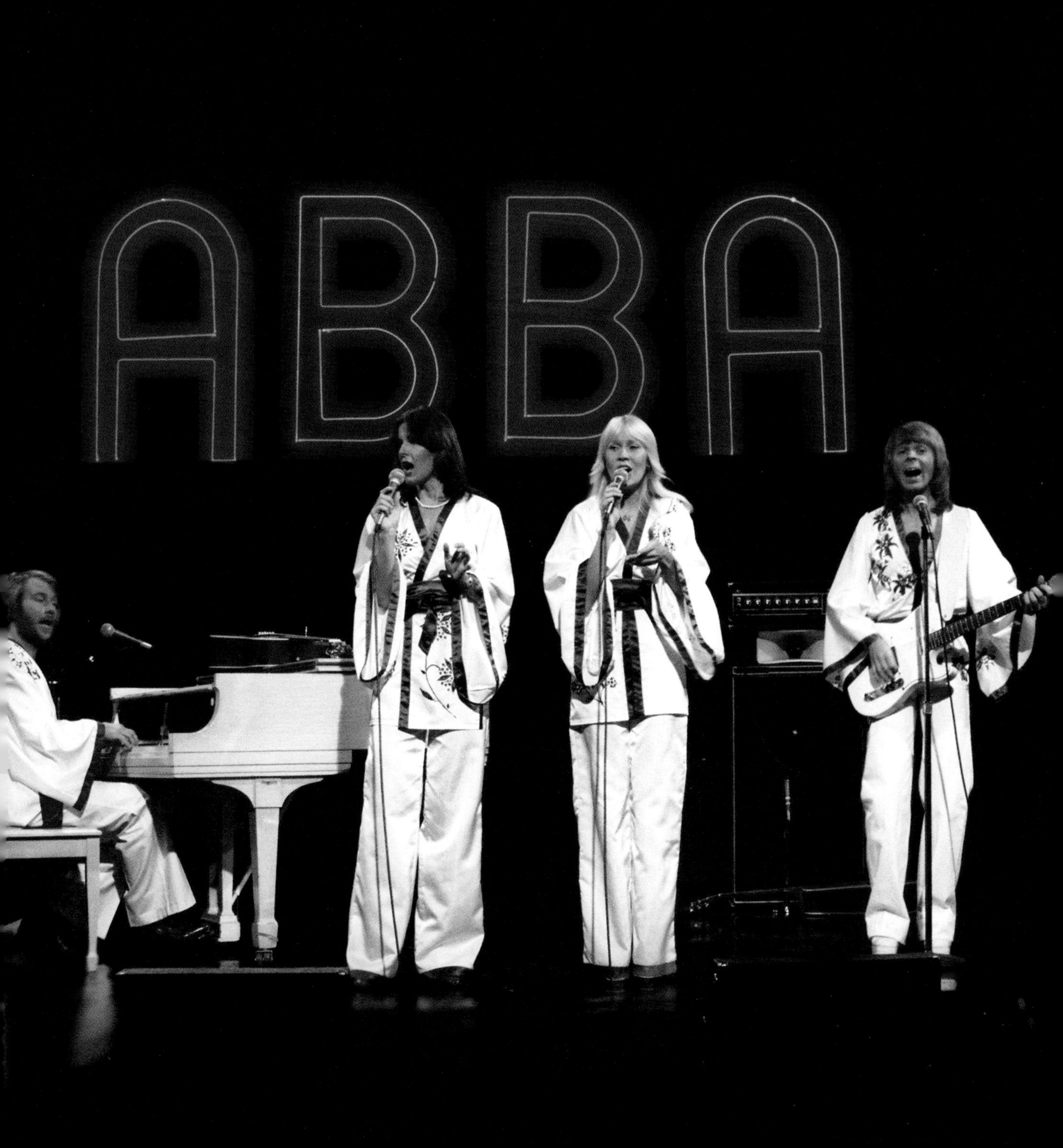
ABBA

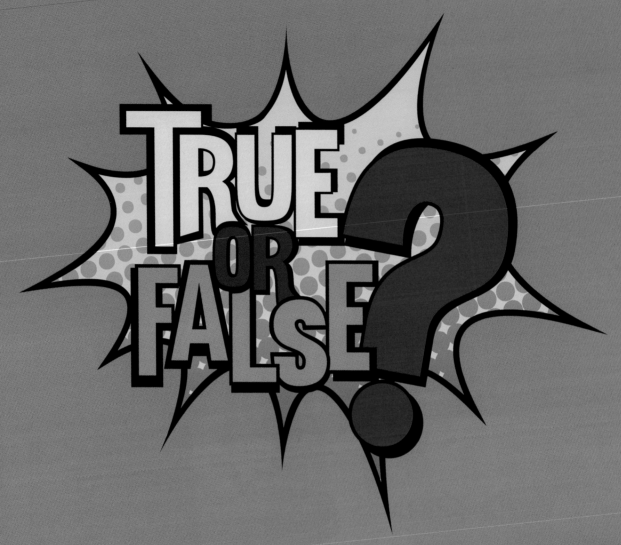

At age 16, the Canadian singer Justin Bieber in 2010 became the youngest solo male artist to top the *Billboard* albums chart.

In 1963, 13-year-old American singer **Stevie Wonder** became the youngest solo male artist to top the chart, with *Recorded Live: The 12 Year Old Genius*. **Bieber** became the second youngest male solo artist to top the chart with *My World 2.0* in 2010.

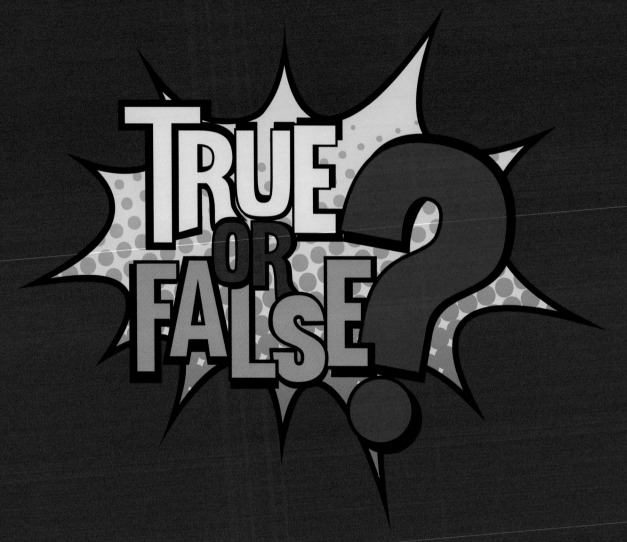

An African American musician caused a stir in 2019 when his rap song became a country music hit.

Lil Nas X's "Old Town Road" caused controversy in the music industry when it appeared on *Billboard*'s Hot Country Songs chart. The song blends elements of rap and hip-hop music with tones and themes from country music.

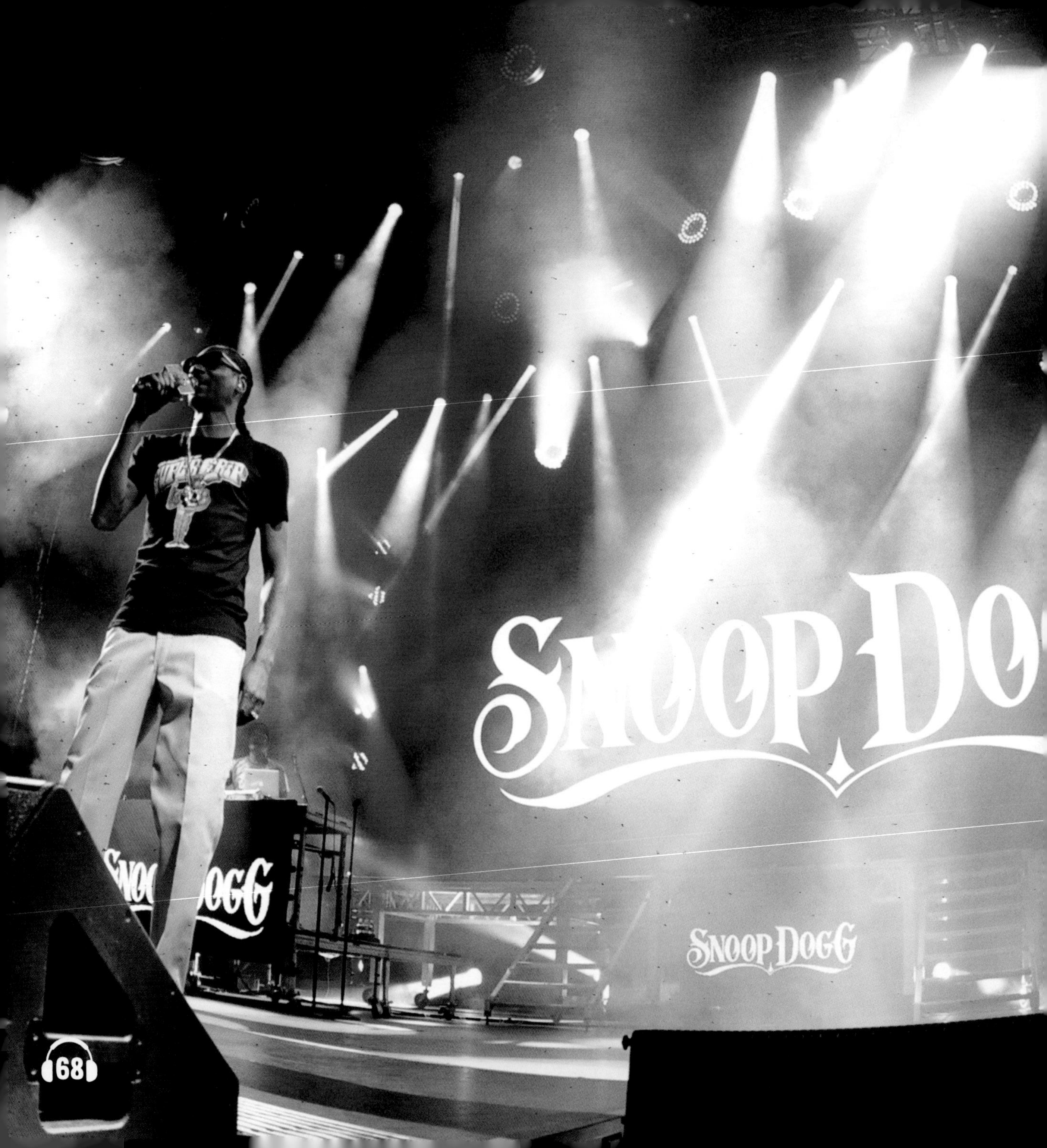
SNOOP DOGG

TRUE OR FALSE?

The American rap artist Snoop Dogg got his stage name because he looked like the cartoon character Snoopy from the comic strip "Peanuts."

Snoop Dogg's real name is Cordozar Calvin Broadus. His mother gave him the nickname Snoopy as a child because she thought he looked like the cartoon's famous beagle character.

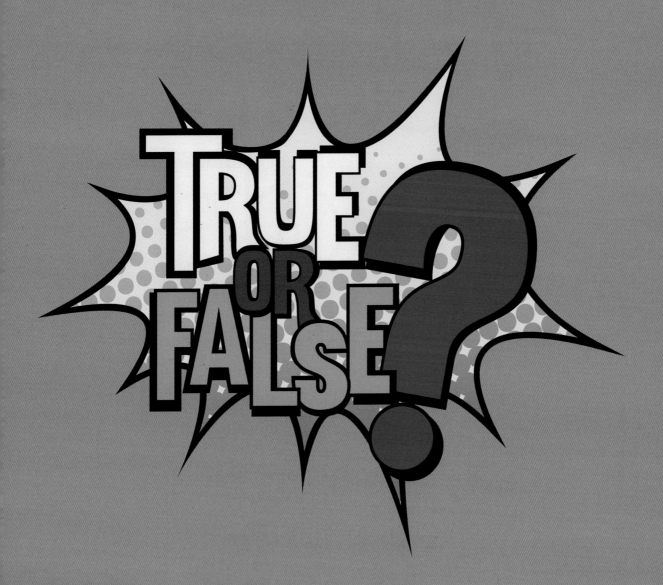

TRUE OR FALSE?

Taylor Swift's album *Fearless* (2008) became the first album by a woman artist to sell more than 7 million copies.

Madonna's album *Like a Virgin* (1984) became the first album by a woman artist to sell more than 7 million copies. It included the hit single "Material Girl." Swift's *Fearless* also went on to sell more than 7 million copies.

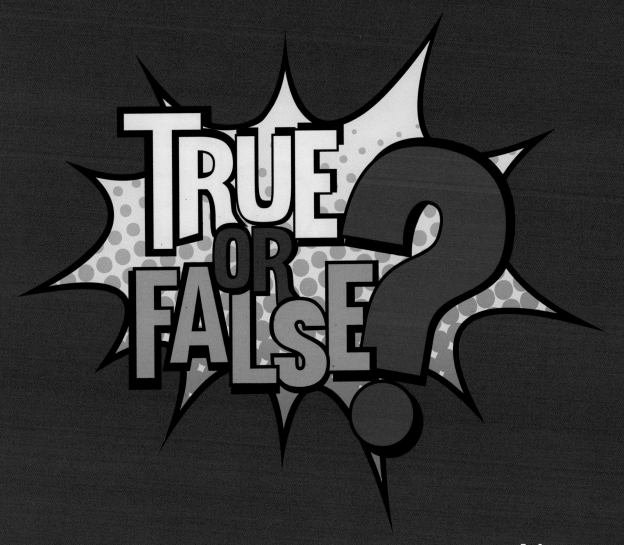

TRUE OR FALSE?

The Grammy Awards were named in honor of the grandmother of the first president of the National Academy of Recording Arts & Sciences.

Grammy comes from the word *gramophone*. A gramophone is an early type of *phonograph* (record player). The Grammy Awards honor excellence in the recording arts and sciences.

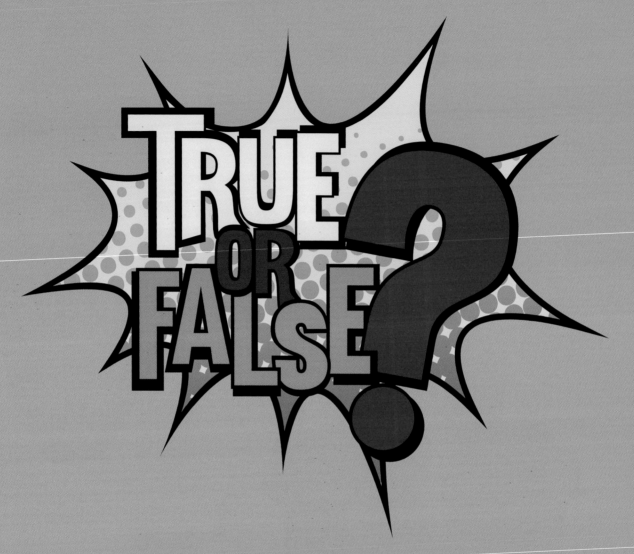

The American singer Beyoncé is the most nominated woman in Grammy history.

TRUE!

Beyoncé Giselle Knowles has been
nominated for more than 50 Grammy
Awards in her career. Queen Bey has
also won a number of Grammys.

TRUE OR FALSE?

NASA sent a cosmic "playlist" into outer space for aliens to listen to.

THE
SOUNDS
OF
EARTH

Side 1

NASA

UNITED STATES OF AMERICA
PLANET EARTH

85

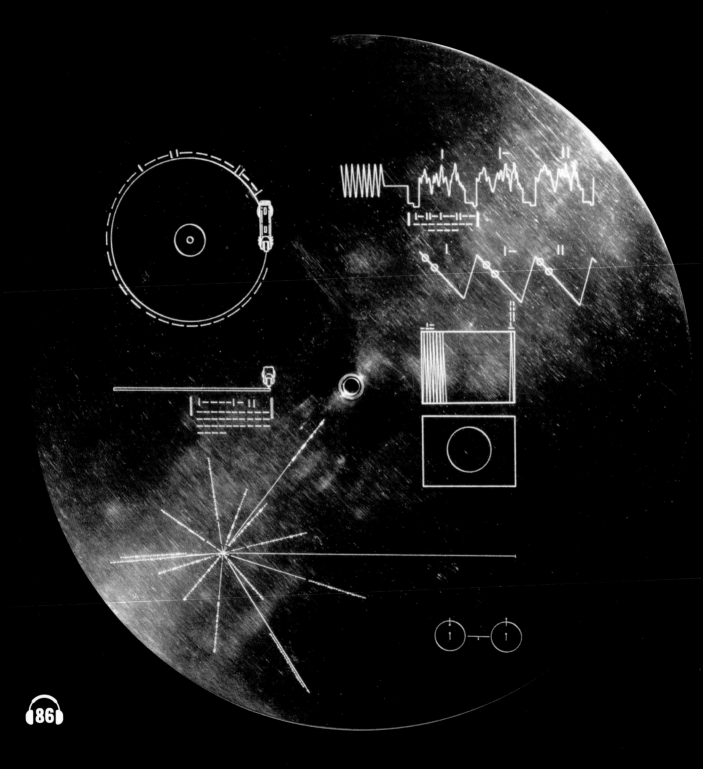

TRUE!

In 1977, NASA launched a series of recordings into outer space aboard the Voyager spacecraft. The recordings contain sounds and images selected to portray the diversity of life and culture on Earth. Maybe aliens are rocking out to pop music in outer space!

TRUE OR FALSE?

If you are a rap artist and you "drop the mic," you are very clumsy.

If you are a rapper and you "drop the *mic* (microphone)," it means you have finished your performance and you are triumphant! But you shouldn't really drop the mic—microphones are fragile and expensive!

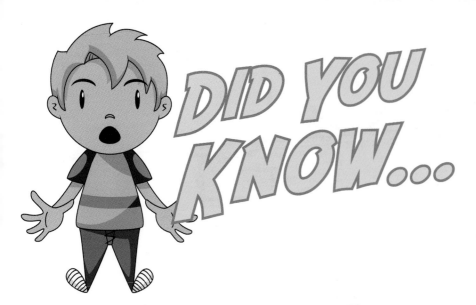

DID YOU KNOW...

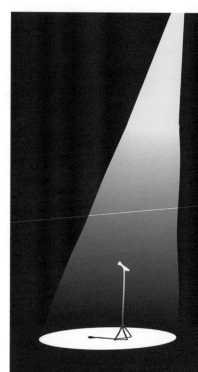

Christina Aguilera, Britney Spears, and Justin Timberlake all performed on "The All New Mickey Mouse Club" television series as children.

ABBA, Céline Dion, the Spanish singer Julio Iglesias, and the English-born Australian singer Olivia Newton-John all competed on the Eurovision Song Contest annual singing competition.

Rock-N-Roll

Elvis Presley

In 2015, Adele's single "Hello" became the first song to sell over **1 million downloads in a week.**

Elvis Presley was **working as a truck driver** when he made his first record in 1954 at age 18.

The Canadian singer Shawn Mendes became famous after posting online a brief clip of himself singing a Justin Bieber tune.

Index

Acknowledgments

Cover: © File 404/Shutterstock; © Ovchynnikov Oleksii,
        Shutterstock; © Iarionova Olga 11/Shutterstock

5-19   © Shutterstock
21   Walt Disney TV/ABC (licensed under CC BY-ND 2.0)
22   Justin Higuchi (licensed under CC BY 2.0)
25-33   © Shutterstock
34   © Ray Mickshaw, Getty Images
36   © Kraft74/Shutterstock
39   © Justin Sullivan, Getty Images
40-51   © Shutterstock
53   © Vinnie Zuffante, Getty Images
55   © Timothy A. Clary, Getty Images
56   © Kraft74/Shutterstock
59   © Michael Ochs Archives/Getty Images
61   © Kathy Hutchins, Shutterstock
63   © Archive Photos/Getty Images
65   © Denise Truscello, Getty Images
67   © Matt Winkelmeyer, Getty Images
68   © Jack Fordyce, Shutterstock
71   © Bennett Raglin, Getty Images; © Peanuts
72-83   © Shutterstock
85-86   NASA/JPL-Caltech
89-93   © Shutterstock